ADVAN

"I am not sure which word is most important in the title of this book.

- *Simplified*: Jennifer does a supreme job of reducing this topic to the critical and actionable components.

- *Cybersecurity:* This is very consumable and therefore easy to share with prospects.

- *Selling*: Pages of action items will improve your practice.

Any salesperson could learn from this book—an MSP can thrive from the advice!"

—MARNIE STOCKMAN, CEO, *Lifecycle Insights*

"Jennifer's book is pure gold! It is truly a step-by-step playbook for MSPs to master the art of selling cyber-security. Many books are generic sales guides, but Jennifer's is targeted at MSPs and selling cyber-security. It was so good I was literally taking notes as I read page after page. This is a MUST READ for all MSPs. Well done!"

—ART GROSS, CEO, *Breach Secure Now*

"Most MSPs struggle with sales. As cybersecurity threats grow, the sales challenge becomes even more difficult. This book is exactly what MSPs need to crack the cybersecurity sales code. Jennifer is an amazing sales pro, and her advice on how to sell cybersecurity is spot on and highly actionable."

—BRIAN FREISTAT, *Vertical Axion*

"Intuitively, I knew that selling cybersecurity was different than selling managed services. But until reading this book, I didn't understand how different they really are. Jennifer does a terrific job articulating how different these sales are, why discovery is so important when selling cybersecurity, and why you will fail if you try to sell cybersecurity using the same tactics and benefits of selling your managed services. This is a must read if you want to be uber successful getting your customers (and prospects) to pay extra for the security they need."

—MARK WINTER, *RapidFire Tools*

"This book speaks the MSP language, so you will read examples that make sense to you! It isn't Jennifer saying, 'There is one way to sell.' She brings together the best of breed of sales methodologies to help you. It's fast paced, easy to understand and an incredible resource for anyone looking to improve their sales game—which means everyone should read it!"

—MATT SOLOMON, Co-Founder, *Channel Program*

BONUS RESOURCES

As a special "thank you gift" for my readers,
I'm sharing some extra resources
to make it even simpler for you
to sell cybersecurity!

Previously for private clients only,
now you can get access, too.

SIMPLIFIED CYBERSECURITY SALES FOR MSPs

THE SECRET FORMULA FOR CLOSING CYBERSECURITY DEALS WITHOUT FEELING SLIMY

JENNIFER BLEAM

To all the people who saw greatness in me years before I saw it in myself.

Thank you for your patience, tough love, guidance, support, and kindness.

I'm so grateful for you.

Special thanks to these remarkable people:

Alex B.
Dan
Jay
Alex R.
Barb E.
Alex S.
Dawn R.
And dozens more

Thank you from the bottom of my heart.

CONTENTS

PART 1

WELCOME

FOREWORD

"Selling." ... "Cybersecurity." Over the past few years, those two simple words (and worlds) have dramatically collided in our industry. The onslaught of hacking and security madness has meant that selling cybersecurity has become a primary focus and need for MSPs. And frankly, to survive and thrive in the next five years, MSPs need to get much, much, *much* better at it.

Not only is this needed because the dark world of cybercrime and hacking is growing rapidly— fueled by positive reinforcement from all the ransomware payouts happening every day—but also because competition in the MSP space is heating up. There are more MSPs than ever before and that number keeps growing.

The MSPs which continually focus on getting better at selling cybersecurity will kill two proverbial birds with one stone. They'll save their clients from almost certain doom and disaster and they'll profit generously from doing so, making sure the future of their clients' businesses is safe.

However, one of the most common patterns I see from working with thousands of MSPs around the world is that while the vast majority of them are *amazing* at building technical solutions, they are downright *horrible* at selling them.

Don't get me wrong. I completely understand. In the first few years of trying to build my MSP, I was the *worst salesperson on the planet.* I'm not joking. I lost deal after deal because I was an awkward, bumbling, unorganized mess. I had to wear white shirts to meetings just so no one would see the horrible nervous sweat marks!

It took me the better part of a decade to become confident in sales meetings, happy to present to boards and excited to pitch and promote my MSP offerings. I had to re-wire a bunch of bad beliefs about myself and perhaps more importantly, I had to rewire a bunch of beliefs around what selling is all about.

In hindsight, this was one of the most transformational and worthwhile upgrades I made to myself in my lifetime. Being able to confidently sell—and believing 150% that what you're doing is right—is an incredibly powerful skill both in business and in life. The feeling you get when you respectfully sell a business owner something that is going to dramatically improve their world or save their hard work from almost certain ruin is exhilarating, exciting, and very, very fulfilling.

And right now, in this current cybercrime landscape, I believe building confidence at respectfully selling cybersecurity offerings is the most important and highest leveraged skill an MSP owner (and their team) could work on. In fact, if there's one single belief I'd love to see *every MSP* in the world have, it's this:

"I believe it's our *absolute* duty to be *wildly* confident at *passionately* selling our *amazing* cybersecurity offerings to businesses, because by doing so, we will very likely *save* their business (and their livelihood) from almost certain doom and disaster."

Imagine how different the IT landscape would be right now if every single MSP owner held this belief deeply at the core of everything they (and their team) do. There would be far fewer hacks and far more secure businesses out there. Businesses would make smarter decisions and invest more into cybersecurity (and technology in general) because they were being *passionately* educated and *confidently* served by MSPs who deeply believed in their mission.

For the people (aka humans) involved, this would result in far less anxiety, far less family problems, and far less mental health issues... because these are the real outcomes of cybercrime.

Unfortunately though, the current landscape is summed up more like this:

"Most (if not all) businesses that have been hit by a cyberattack unfortunately hadn't (yet) had a conversation with an MSP who felt it was their *absolute* duty to be *wildly* confident at *passionately* selling their *amazing* cybersecurity offerings. If they had, they very likely would not have become a *victim*."

Read that sentence again. I want it to sink in.

You see, your primary duty as an MSP has shifted from the simple *"We help businesses with technology issues"* to the much more important *"We help businesses get the most out of technology whilst keeping them as secure as possible."*

Doctors and nurses go to work every day to save humans from disease and death and to help them live a healthier life. It's why they wake up in the morning. Your mission as an MSP is to save businesses from hackers and disaster and to help them better use technology to become more profitable, efficient, and innovative.

It's a noble mission. To do it though, you *must be good at selling* (the right way).

And today, you're in luck.

In your hands is a book with a framework that will help you collapse time and rapidly upgrade your skillset to become world-class at *selling cyber-security*. Where my sales confidence upgrade took me the better part of a decade, you'll be able to build the same skills, beliefs and confidence in only days and weeks.

I've known Jennifer for a number of years, and I've been encouraging her to write this book to share her amazing passion and deep wisdom for the cybersecurity selling process. I wanted more MSPs to benefit from her knowledge. So, when she finally told me she'd made the decision to do it, I was *pumped!*

The reason it took me the better part of a decade to go from a *bumbling buffoon* to a *confident seller* is because I didn't have mentors like Jennifer in my world who wrote books like this. She's not only one of the world's best at selling cybersecurity, she's also one of the world's best at teaching *you* how to get better at it *yourself*. And, more importantly, she's passionate about doing just that.

Right now, I can say with "hand on heart" that I don't know any other way an MSP can better equip themselves with the skills, confidence, and framework to *confidently* and *respectfully* sell their cybersecurity offerings than by devouring all the tips, tricks, and wisdom Jennifer has packed into these pages.

I know one of the standard statements people write in a book's Foreword is "This book is essential reading," and a lot of the time it's just that person blowing hot air to inflate the author's ego. However, in this case this book truly is *essential reading for every MSP,* not because I want to inflate Jennifer's (very humble) ego, but because I truly, deeply, and confidently believe it.

Now it's your turn. Flip the page and devour this thing!

Then give a copy to everyone on your team. Your current and future clients *need* you to.

NIGEL MOORE
Founder of The Tech Tribe
Former MSP Owner

WHO SHOULD READ THIS BOOK

Even though this is a short book, designed to be read in an hour or so, I don't want to waste *any* of your time if it's not a good fit. Please take a few minutes and read this entire section to see if *Simplified Cybersecurity Sales For MSPs* is a good use of your time. Because time is your most precious asset, I never want to take it for granted.

I wrote this short book for 3 specific reasons:

1. To give you a high-level overview of sales

2. To show you how to apply sales fundamentals to cybersecurity sales specifically

3. To give you confidence that you (yes, you!) can sell cybersecurity easily and effectively

I am a straight-shooter kind of coach, so I'm comfortable saying this: While I truly want to serve the MSP and MSSP community, and while I want you to learn to sell cybersecurity effectively, I also want some of my readers to reach out to me to see if working together makes sense.

At its core, this is a book about sales. And you would likely think I was a poor excuse for a sales coach if I didn't make a "next step" offer... for qualified readers.

Since my best clients are looking for any edge to help them save time and money—and avoid common mistakes—this book will deliver that edge. Then (spoiler alert!) I hope I've built enough "know, like, and trust" throughout the pages of this short book so that you just may choose to take me up on my offer for the logical next step.

But for now, don't even worry about the next step. If you're okay with that premise (at least in theory), let me dig specifically into who I wrote this book for and who can benefit most from its content. That way you can determine if you should continue to read this book—or if you should put it down and read something else!

I believe that every MSP and IT professional should be selling cybersecurity services. But there are two specific types of people who should read this book:

1. **The salesperson**. If you wear the sales hat in your organization—whether as your full-time job or one of many roles, this book is for you. You *must* know how to

demonstrate the value of cybersecurity to your prospects (and clients). This shows up in how your discovery conversations are crafted, how you recognize and respond to objections, and how you iterate and improve your sales process and sales conversations.

2. **The sales manager**. If at least one member of the sales team reports to you, you should read this book, too. You are responsible for encouraging your team's success. You must have an above-average understanding of sales and how to sell cybersecurity. Otherwise, you will lose your team's respect—and the worst employees might even try to take advantage of you.

So if you are a salesperson or a sales manager and you want to become even more effective at selling cybersecurity, then read on. Because this book is for you.

MY PROMISE TO YOU

I promise to make *Simplified Cybersecurity Sales For MSPs* a valuable use of your money, time, and attention. Within the next 60 to 90 minutes, my goal is to open your eyes to a world of possibility in cybersecurity sales, to show you how easy (and possible) it is for you to sell cybersecurity, and to motivate you to take action toward becoming an amazing salesperson.

I will minimize the filler and get right to the point. I'll share exactly what you need to know to sell cybersecurity successfully. In other words, I wrote this book the way I wish all books were written—concise, cut-to-the-chase content that assumes I'm smart enough to fill in a few blanks.

Before we move too far, I want to be clear. I am not going to spend any time helping you build your cybersecurity stack. There are other books and training courses that can help you reach that goal. Today I'm making the assumption that you have a security solution you believe in, and that it will (really and truly) deliver risk mitigation.

If you're hoping I can help you prove the value of a half-baked solution, give you confidence in that wimpy stack, or show you a magic way to pull the wool over your prospects' eyes, this is *not* the book for you.

On the other hand, if you are looking for concrete ways to prove the value of your cybersecurity services and engage in (sometimes difficult) client conversations, I am 100% convinced this is the right book for you.

INTRODUCTION

———————|———————

If you're reading this book, you have accepted the mission to protect your clients. Selling cyber-security is a significant opportunity because it is such a significant need. If that need is not filled, countless small and medium-sized businesses will be significantly impacted by cyber threats, and the impact will ripple through the global economy.

But if you have not made the time to become good at selling cybersecurity, you are doing a disservice to your clients and to yourself. The future of your business and your clients' businesses depends on the content of this book. I invite you to rise to this challenge and learn to sell cybersecurity.

Selling is the lifeblood of your business, the engine of your business vehicle. What gasoline does for your car, sales does for your business. Selling is mandatory. Arguably, it is more important than having standard operating procedures, hiring manuals, and financial processes. None of those processes and procedures matter in the least if you don't have any clients.

Robert Herjavec, star of *Shark Tank* and CEO of a global IT security firm states, "You must wake up every morning and sell something." Today is that morning. Let's get to work!

Cybersecurity is different from other managed services... because your prospects believe a threat won't happen to them.

So why read a book about cybersecurity sales? Simply put, cybersecurity sales is different from managed services. Chances are, you have largely figured out your managed service sales process, even if it's not fully documented and you're not consistently able to execute on it. Even without a written sales playbook, making a managed services sale has come relatively easily to you in the past few years.

However, selling cybersecurity is very different. It is even more intangible than managed services. It is not something your prospects can relate to, because they don't understand what cybersecurity is. When you ask prospects to invest in cyber-security, not only is it invisible to them, but they believe they aren't even vulnerable to its equally invisible threat. So why would they part with their hard-earned money?

Yet we know they absolutely are vulnerable. It is our job to somehow convince them that they are at risk and that they must invest now. And that's really the crux of the issue: they must not put off a decision. You absolutely must demonstrate urgency. Otherwise, prospects will put you off. They'll wait until tomorrow, next month, next quarter, or next year. They'll wait until their business has a breach or a ransomware attack or an incident. Then they will blame you for their own inaction.

It is crucial that they invest now, to reduce the likelihood of this disaster happening. And that is why it is crucial for you to read this book right now—because you cannot wait until next week, next month, next quarter, or next year to learn this valuable skill.

As an extra benefit, learning to sell cybersecurity well will make you better at selling managed services, co-managed IT, or compliance services— because sales fundamentals don't change.

Throughout this book, you'll be introduced to various concepts and examples that will help you become a better salesperson. Even more importantly, you'll see why selling cybersecurity is one of the most important skills you must develop. If you need additional support, please feel free to email me at jennifer@mspsalesrevolution.com. I'm always happy to lend support in any way I can.

PART 2

SALES OVERVIEW

1 | ONE OF THESE THINGS IS NOT LIKE THE OTHER

When I first started my sales coaching business, one of my colleagues asked, "Why are you coaching cybersecurity sales? Sales is sales. Cybersecurity sales isn't any different from managed services sales." I answered, "Well, cybersecurity sales may not seem different to you, but it absolutely is different."

To be clear, sales fundamentals never change. Inside of my mentorship program, I constantly remind my clients to practice sales essentials consistently. There are fundamental truths regardless of whether you're selling managed services, cybersecurity, co-managed, compliance, or even purple umbrellas. (As an aside, if you're selling purple umbrellas, I'd love to find out how you've woven that into your managed services business...)

EXPERIENCE

Even so, selling cybersecurity is different from selling managed services. For one thing, most people reading this book have only a little experience selling cybersecurity. It is new. And that makes it uncomfortable. You don't have any muscle memory. And because you have little experience with it, you must think about every step. It's easy to get thrown off track; it feels hard.

> *Learning to sell cybersecurity will make you even better at selling other managed services.*

I've had the "joy" of teaching two of my sons to drive. One was methodical and measured with his driving habits. It turned out he'd been studying my driving for the past few months in preparation for this big moment. My other son... well, let's just say he had not studied. He couldn't remember to use the turn signal. He frequently got the brake and the gas pedals confused. And there was even this one time where he drove down the sidewalk instead of the road (on my husband's watch).

Here's my point. Now that my oldest two sons have been driving for a few years, it comes easily. They can drive while listening to music, talking to their friends, and chewing gum. It's not hard anymore. It's almost enjoyable. But when starting out, it felt almost impossible.

If selling cybersecurity feels difficult today, rest assured that you will develop the skills needed to sell cyber effectively—as long as you put in time and effort.

RETURN ON INVESTMENT

Another way that selling security services is different from selling managed services is related to Return On Investment (ROI). When I first started selling managed services, conversations were simple. The prospect was trading dollars for increased productivity and profitability. I went on many sales calls where I would discover prospects who were wasting vast amounts of time.

I remember one sales call vividly. The employee mentioned that she arrived at work on time, but couldn't get started for about 30 minutes. When I asked about the delay, she explained that she would arrive, boot up her computer, go get some coffee, and talk to several colleagues. Then she came back to her desk and sat for a few more minutes—until her computer was ready for her. I discovered that her machine took around 25 minutes to boot up! Then I also found out that she had to reboot at least once per day just to stay functional.

Within that one conversation, I uncovered nearly an hour of wasted time per day. The prospect essentially "bought back" all that time by investing with my managed services company.

But security isn't like that. You can't promise ROI. A business can't spend $100 per employee on cybersecurity and see those dollars returned to them in increased productivity. In fact, you will likely *cost* the company productivity.

No one preaches the need for multi-factor authentication because it makes employees so much more productive. Yet, it's a mandatory part of security.

> *MFA won't make employees more productive... but it's necessary to lower cybersecurity risk!*

Assuming you value honesty and integrity in your sales process, you cannot build a solid security offer and then promise that it will make your clients more efficient. For these reasons (and others) selling cybersecurity is vastly different from selling managed services.

2 | MIND THE GAP

I have studied the art and science of sales for decades. I attended training sessions by CharTec and Gary Pica, and studied under an amazing Sandler trainer for almost two years. I've read hundreds of books about sales, discovery, cold calling, and sales processes in general.

My favorite book by far is *Gap Selling* by Keenan. His methodology works perfectly for cybersecurity sales and managed services sales. He plainly explains how a professional salesperson should conduct their sales calls. This chapter will be a quick synopsis of the three common threads that he teaches throughout his book, translated into language that applies directly to the MSP world when selling cybersecurity.

The first thing you must understand is that there is an inherent gap between where your client is now and where they need to be. And you'll be asking them to move from Point A to Point Z. There is a lot of psychological baggage tied up in the client staying at Point A. Your job is to reveal this gap.

Often the gap is miniscule in the mind of the prospect, when the reality is that it is a Grand Canyon-sized gap. Sometimes the prospect stays at Point A because they made a decision five years ago, and are emotionally tied to justifying it. You must be careful not to insult them by suggesting they made the wrong decision. In fact, the most savvy salespeople will praise the prospect for making a great decision five years ago while simultaneously showing how much has changed since then, and educating the client as to why the past decision no longer serves them.

There is a gap between the cybersecurity services they have now versus what they should have. There is a *vast* difference.

One of the challenges in the sales process is that you already know the gap intuitively. You walk into a sales call with a very good idea of what you're going to find. You already know the prospect is at risk for a major cybersecurity incident. And if you neglect the "Reveal The Gap" thread, your cybersecurity sales tapestry will be meaningless. You will continually try to solve a problem that the prospect does not know they have.

When you "reveal the gap," this means you are revealing it to the prospect. You need to open their eyes to the reality in which they've been living all these years. You must help them realize they should not remain comfortably ignorant; a nightmare scenario is waiting to happen.

> *Don't allow your prospects to remain comfortably ignorant of the cybersecurity nightmare that awaits them.*

The way you do this is through a proper discovery process. Discovery is such an important piece of sales that we will devote an entire chapter to it. Just remember the first thread that needs to be woven throughout your sales tapestry is: You must reveal to your prospect that there actually is a gap.

The second thread inside any successful sales call tapestry is the one I refer to as "Feel The Gap." It is tempting to believe that your client will make decisions logically. You are likely quite analytical. You see a problem, and you find a solution (usually one that involves technology). But if you attempt to present only logical reasons for adopting your cybersecurity solutions, your clients will not buy. Why not? Because people do not buy based on logic. They buy based on emotions.

When you walk into a sales call, your prospect is emotionally invested in staying with their current solutions and their incumbent provider. Helping your prospect feel the gap is where you allow them to feel the emotional significance of the change you want them to make. They must feel why staying at Point A is a bad idea, and emotionally connect to a better feeling in the future you are proposing to them.

Another challenge is that you have firsthand knowledge of how devastating a cyberattack can be. You don't need anyone to spell out the emotional impact of a cybersecurity incident for you. You intuitively feel the gap; you feel how dangerous it is to stay at Point A. You feel how risky it is to do absolutely nothing. You feel how devastatingly impactful a breach will be for this business, possibly causing this business to shut their doors permanently if they change nothing.

Because you feel all of this, you will be tempted to shortcut the discovery process. Resist this temptation! Removing emotion, danger, and risk from the sale means that you have removed their motivation for change. If you falsely assume the prospect sees the danger and already smells the smoke, you won't take the time to yell, "Fire!"

If you feel like you are pushing your prospects toward safety, and they are resistant, it is likely *not* because they are stubborn or cheap, but because they don't know why they should consider moving.

It is imperative to have a conversation with the prospect to help them grasp emotionally how a cyber incident would impact their business. This all happens during the discovery process which we'll dive into deeply in Chapter 5.

Invariably, when I talk to MSPs who have lost a sale, it was because they did a poor job at helping the prospect feel the implications of a cybersecurity incident. Have you ever walked out of a sales call where you *knew* you had the deal in the bag, where the prospect nodded their head in all the right places, where they said, "Sounds great," and then... they ghosted you? Or maybe they opted to stay with their previous provider (who was woefully under-serving them)? It was so clear to you, and the prospect even agreed! Yet they chose to remain in their current state— making zero logical sense to you.

If you've ever experienced this, you need to understand that helping the prospect *feel* the implications of remaining in their current state is a crucial part of your sales calls. Without demonstrating risk, you will not make a sale.

Too many MSPs tell me that clients don't want to buy until after they've had a security incident. The solution to this challenge is to help them feel the agony of that moment now. Everybody makes decisions based on emotion. You must transport prospects to the point of an incident and help them feel the emotion of that moment.

> *You know the impact a cybersecurity incident will cause. Your prospect does not.*

When you master the discovery process and bring the prospect to the moment that they look up at their screen and realize they have been hit with ransomware, then you can begin to mitigate that risk.

Before that point, first you helped the prospect understand that there was a gap which must be addressed (Reveal The Gap), and now you have helped them understand how leaving that gap unattended would feel in the midst of a cyber-security incident (Feel The Gap).

The third and final thread, which will allow you to complete this beautiful sales tapestry, is to make the sale. This thread, where you help the prospect Heal The Gap, allows them to mitigate the risk of a devastating breach or attack. This thread, closing the sale, is so crucial—and so misunderstood—that we dedicated Chapter 11 to exploring this concept thoroughly. For now, understand that in order to Heal The Gap, you must have woven the other two threads masterfully. If you did not, you will push for the sale and likely be unsuccessful.

These three common threads should be woven throughout the tapestry of every sales call. It's now quite easy to debrief a sales call:

1. Did you help every person in the room realize there was a gap?

2. How many business implications did you help them internalize? Every person in the room should have at least 2-4 ways that a cyber incident could impact their job role or their team.

3. And then finally, did you ask for the sale?

3 | BACK TO BASICS

Whether you are a seasoned sales professional, or brand new to the amazing world of sales, it is important to understand sales fundamentals. There are ten critical fundamentals that you must keep in mind during every sales interaction.

1. CONTROL

Many sales books talk about tiny details like setting a clear next step, using an upfront contract, or driving the sales conversation. To be sure, these details are important. But the underlying principle at play is that you must control the sales process. (Of course, this assumes that you have a process, which we'll cover in detail in future chapters.)

It is your job to control the pace of the conversation, your prospect's emotions, and the direction of the sales call. You should never wander aimlessly around, hoping to eventually end up at the point where you get a check or a commitment.

It is your job as a professional salesperson to steer the conversation, to control the question flow, and to anticipate answers.

2. DO WHAT'S IN THE BEST INTEREST OF THE CLIENT

If you've ever felt like a slimy salesperson, then this mantra (a favorite of mine) will help. The best MSPs have assembled a great cybersecurity offer, and it is in the best interest of the client to adopt it. (It is also in the IT pro's best interest to learn how to sell the offer, which is why you're reading this book.)

Whenever you are tempted to create a "low-tier" security offer, or remove pieces of your current offering, remember this critical rule:

*If it's not in the
best interest of the client,
you should not do it.*

3. LISTEN

We humans like to talk... a lot. And when someone listens to us, we feel heard and valued. We also start to trust the listener.

Your job is to listen. When your prospect talks a lot, it means they like you. Your goal is to craft questions that elicit long, thoughtful responses. This means that you need to create great discovery questions and be a good listener.

You won't be able to create these off the top of your head. You'll need to study questions and determine what works best. You'll want to review your sales calls and determine what questions only received a one-word answer and replace those questions in the future. Your goal is to get prospects to open up to you. Your job is to listen.

4. FOLLOW UP

As a professional salesperson, you must follow up. Now I understand this seems to be in direct contradiction to Fundamental #1, where you were reminded to always stay in control. But there will be times where you don't always maintain control. Perhaps you forgot to set a firm next step during your first sales call. Perhaps your prospect stood you up on that next call. Perhaps you delivered a proposal and the prospect wanted to run the agreement past their attorney. Never passively wait for your prospect to come running to you, check in hand, begging to do business with you. While that might happen one or two times during your career, it is *far* from the norm. This means it will take discipline to follow up on your leads, your prospects, and your contacts. Follow-up is crucial to your success.

5. Discovery is Key

One of the biggest jobs of a professional salesperson is to help the prospect realize they are under-served. The best way to do this is during the discovery process, where you demonstrate that there is a gap between how the prospect is being served today and what their world *should* look like. Discovery is likely the most misunderstood and marginalized part of sales, so we will be devoting an entire chapter to this critical sales fundamental.

6. Always Ask for the Sale

If the sale is in the best interest of the client, ask for it. I see a common thread when I debrief my clients' sales calls. Often I'll get to the end of the review and realize they didn't ask for the sale. They didn't roll into explaining their onboarding process (assuming the sale). They just stopped. They presented the challenges in the network today; they explained how the prospect would be better served with them. And they stopped. Remember: most prospects will not beg you to take their money. You must always ask for the sale.

7. Have (and Follow) a Documented Sales Process

It is crucial to have a sales process. In fact, companies with a documented sales process close more sales and make more money than companies who don't have a documented process. Now, even if you don't have a sales process that is fully documented, you do have a process. And that process is delivering exactly the results that the process is designed to deliver. However, if you are not closing at least 60% of your sales, then your process is not optimized. If you're only closing 20% or 30% of qualified leads, then that is because of your process. So let's fix the process.

8. Defuse Objections

It is so tempting to walk into a sales call, cross your fingers, and hope that you won't hear your most hated objection. If you have a "least favorite" objection, then you'll want to take a look at Chapter 8, where we will talk about objection handling in great detail. But for now, recognize that you must have a response for every objection you have ever heard. When you hear an objection for the first time, then of course, you aren't expected to defuse it. But if you hear the same objection during a second sales call and are caught flat-footed again, that's a fail on your part.

9. EMOTION

Sales is a transfer of emotion. Every human being makes decisions emotionally. But sometimes prospects need some encouragement from you to make that last step. Transfer your confidence to your prospect. Speak passionately about how you can solve their problems; remind them of the problems they didn't even know about until you arrived. Reiterate the future state you'll deliver and how this solution is exactly what they need. Of course, this means you must maintain your own emotional state so that you can have that emotion ready to be able to transfer to your prospect.

10. REVIEW YOUR SALES CALLS

I highly encourage you to record your sales calls, if that's legal for you. This allows you to go back and debrief those sales calls later. (Recordings are so much better than your memory!)

To create a debrief checklist, list these ten fundamentals. Did you follow them? What was one objection that you could have handled better? What was one place in your sales call where you knocked it out of the park? (Go study that or even memorize it.)

Professional sports teams review their game films weekly. Imagine how poor your favorite team would be if they never looked at their own game films. If they didn't review when a play went right or wrong, they wouldn't recognize missed opportunities. They never realized that a play looked great on paper, but never quite worked in real life.

Sports teams improve by analyzing their game films. And salespeople improve by analyzing their sales calls.

Make sure you are following the fundamentals. These fundamentals are how you get 1% better every day. That's how you iterate and improve on what was previously your best. And by the way, if you have a goal to hire a salesperson, recorded sales calls and debriefs are an extremely helpful training tool. So not only is recording and debriefing those sales calls important for you in the short-term, but as you start to scale your team, they become important long-term as well.

4 | WHY HAVE A PROCESS

In the words of W. Edwards Deming, "Every system is perfectly designed to get the results it gets." In other words, cause-and-effect drives your process, or lack of process, and directly influences the results you will see.

This principle applies to marketing and customer service. And of course sales. This means that if you don't like your sales results, you must change your sales process. This is the heart of your process improvement document. Make a list of what you're doing today, track the results, and then iterate. Did your results improve? If so, that process becomes your control.

Then iterate again. A valid sales process is a work in progress due to shifting challenges. It develops as you adjust to challenges you encounter. Of course, if you encounter challenges but don't recognize or pay attention to them during your sales calls, then you will never improve your sales process. And if that remains the case, you will never improve your sales results. So make sure you are paying attention to your sales calls.

I call this "debriefing your sales calls." It simply means going back and documenting what happened. Did you follow your process? Yes, this assumes that you have a process, and if you don't, then it's time to go back to the previous step of writing down what you normally do in a sales call.

While debriefing your sales calls, also consider where your process may have fallen short or where you might have become uncomfortable during the call. Did you encounter objections that surprised you? How can you change your process so those objections don't happen again?

What objections did you hear for the second time that should have already been addressed by a previous update to your process?

Did you get a firm next step from the prospect or client?

What was one part of your sales call that you absolutely dominated? Make note of anything that you explained particularly well or where the words just flowed clearly and smoothly. Document this like a script and memorize it as best as you can.

This debriefing process will help you to make changes before you develop bad habits. It will also allow you to recognize where you might have been deviating from your process, or where your process needs to be improved.

So, as you create your process and then iterate it, here are some of the typical challenges MSPs face:

1. The prospect says, "I need to think about it." Then they ghost you.

2. You get partway through the discovery or risk assessment process only to find out that your point of contact is not the decision maker.

3. Your prospect has champagne tastes on a beer budget. In other words, they do not have two dimes to rub together, but they love everything you're telling them.

4. Your prospect does not care at all about cybersecurity, data privacy, or HIPAA compliance in general.

Now, here is part of the magic of a sales process. If you recognize that these examples could happen to you with your current process, then your goal should be to design new segments of your process that will allow you to avoid these circumstances.

Let me give you a real life (non sales) example. When I'm playing chess, one of my weaknesses is that I bring out my queen way too soon. I fall into a trap where I start to believe that she is super powerful and almost invincible. The result of this faulty thinking is that I bring her out into the middle of the board without any protection. When I finally realized this weakness, I designed a process to prevent me from doing that in the future.

My process is very simple. If I'm tempted to move out my queen before other pieces are fairly well-developed, I force myself to resist that temptation at least three times before moving out my queen.

Like sales, this process was iterative. *First, I realized that a weakness existed*—I did not like the outcome of my chess game. When I moved the queen to the center of the board in an unprotected spot, I would always lose. *Next, I developed a strategy* that was simple and worked to prevent me from getting into that situation in the future.

A good sales process allows you to identify weaknesses, gives you space to solve those challenges (outside of the pressure of a real sales call), and reminds you to follow the fundamentals of sales.

To best control your time, you will want to disqualify prospects as early as possible in your sales process. Often when my clients "lose" a sale, it wasn't a viable prospect to begin with. You will never close a non-decision maker. You will almost never close someone who is looking for the cheapest price. And if the prospect has a habit of bouncing from provider to provider, you may not even want them as a client.

Thankfully, all of these situations can be addressed and uncovered. Build this level of detective work into your sales system to allow you to control the process throughout a sales engagement.

As your business scales, and you want to add salespeople, it will be far easier to duplicate a sales process once it is documented. You will be able to equip your new team member with the best possible strategies for success... like using Grandma's famous cookie recipe at a family gathering.

With your sales process, you want to make sure anyone can duplicate your "famous cookie recipe." It needs to be documented in a format that's accessible, and its results need to be reproducible with a minimum of outside explanation.

Here is another truth. It will feel more comfortable to follow the prospect's plan than your own. It may feel exciting at first, because you'll be able to go into those sales calls and be perceived as helpful. You can strut your stuff, play large and in charge, and feed your ego. But the goal of sales is not to feed your ego and feel good about yourself. The goal of sales is to make money.

When you allow yourself to follow your prospect's plan, what happens if your prospect only wants information? What if your prospect only wants the cheapest price? Or the prospect might just be lonely, and simply wants to waste your time, having no intention of making a buying decision.

The goal of sales is always to make money. So you must develop a sales system, a process, that allows you to make money. A viable sales process must culminate in closing the sale.

PART 3

SALES SKILLS
& TECHNIQUES

5 | DISCOVER THE TRUTH
ABOUT DISCOVERY

Discovery. Often this part of the sales process is uncomfortable for MSPs. Meandering and almost useless. You might even be tempted to watch the clock, wondering how short you can make discovery, just to say you did it.

After all, 90% of what you "discover" in sales calls these days is repetitious. The conversations with today's prospect will be Exactly. The. Same. As. Every. Other. Company. In. The. World.

It feels like a complete waste of time. But all the sales gurus insist that discovery is important. So you obediently trudge through this step, eager to get to the fun part—the part where you can ride in like a knight on a gleaming white horse and solve your prospects' problems!

This chapter will reveal a simple shift that will radically alter the effectiveness of your sales process and increase your close rate! Are you ready for the change? Brace yourself. Here we go:

DISCOVERY IS FOR THE PROSPECT

Discovery is not for you. Discovery is for the prospect. Yes, it's that simple. Truly. Because (as you've already experienced) you're not going to "discover" much at all. You're an absolute fortune teller!

You already know that:

- Their backups haven't been tested

- Anti-virus is missing on at least one machine, and probably the server

- They're missing patches

- There will be data scattered all over their network (inside of software tools that "no one" knew were there)

- Passwords are being reused

- Accounts are not being decommissioned correctly

- The incumbent provider told them they had all the security they needed. You'll likely discover a free antivirus tool and a firewall (you hope)

- Blah blah blah. The list goes on forever! (But it's the same story in almost every company.)

But here's the reality—and don't miss this: Your prospects don't know any of this. And more importantly, they don't care... yet. They don't know that these problems are happening in their business, and they don't see how these issues could impact their future. And *that* is why discovery is critically important.

Your job (during discovery) is to help *them* discover these issues, and also to discover that, if left unresolved, these shortcomings could significantly alter all their future plans, including their day-to-day business functionality. They also need to discover that there are ways to mitigate these threats.

With general IT-related problems, you need to take your prospects through a progression:

- First, you'll help them discover that a problem exists (in general, in the world today).

- Then, they'll discover (with your expert guidance) that a problem exists inside of their own company right now.

- Then you'll guide them to the most important discovery of all: how that problem will impact them.

Now sometimes companies have solid networks in place. But they are still under-protected. With cybersecurity risks that could occur (an incident, a ransomware attack, or a breach), the progression is a little different. You must help your prospects discover as many of these realities as possible:

- They must discover that cyber threats exist (in general).

- Then, they must discover that this problem happens to SMBs (small businesses) and not just bigger firms.

- And they *also* must discover that cyber events happen locally (to companies in your town, county, or niche).

- Additionally you must help them discover the impact to them personally, to specific parts of their company, and to their brand or reputation at large.

Pretend you are an attorney making a case for your cybersecurity solution. While you don't have to make every point every time, the more of these points that you can prove, the easier your sales job will become.

And each of these points is about helping the prospect *discover* a little more of the truth.

Discovery, as you now see, is for *them*, not for you.

Your job is that of a guide. You guide them down a path that is familiar to you; you simply help them discover truth along the way.

Your goal is to use the discovery process to help a prospect *discover* that the probability of something happening is high and that the impact on their business can be catastrophic. Your job is to craft questions that will prove these two arguments.

Here are some concrete ways to accomplish this.

Discover that a threat exists (in general).

- "Can you tell me about your current process to keep ransomware out of your company?"

There likely will be zero processes in place. You may even want to ask if they've heard of ransomware. Are they familiar with what it is? Then give a gentle recap statement. "So you kind of knew it was a thing, but you don't really have a good strategy in place to keep it out. Okay. I understand." And then move on.

Discover that it happens to SMBs and not just bigger firms.

- "It's really interesting. So many companies that I talk to see cybersecurity in the news—like the pipeline attacks or major hotel chains hit with ransomware or things like that. Since the news only talks about larger companies being affected, there's a tendency to believe that a cyber incident can't happen to small business owners. Do you feel like small business owners are vulnerable to cyberattacks?"

- "Most of the companies I talk to are surprised to learn <insert a relevant, up-to-date statistic about small businesses in your region, niche, etc.>. Do you find that surprising, too?"

Discover that it happens locally (to companies in your town, county, or niche).

- "I'm curious. Did you see the story about <local small business>?"

HINT: Find a local story that contains a public interest section. Typically this will include an interview with an executive. They will usually talk about all the challenges of not being able to access data, how they thought a cyber event would never happen to them, and how awful it's been and how there's no end in sight.

- "The part of this story that is so heart-breaking to me is this section right here. She talks about losing money and the stress of not sleeping for days. And all of this risk could have been mitigated."

Discover the impact to them personally (if they do nothing) and the impact if they address the gap.

- "It sounds like being dead in the water for three weeks is a risk you'd like to avoid. Is that fair?"

- "So if we did nothing, and a cyber incident occurred, would you be the one to personally call your top 40 clients, or would you delegate that to someone else?" (Demonstrate personal impact.)

- "And who would talk to the press and your attorney?" (Demonstrate personal impact or impact to another team member.)

- "It would probably mean a sleepless night or two? (I remember when I was younger, those all-nighters were a lot easier than they are now!)"

- "Transparently, this is one of the more uncomfortable parts of my job as your outsourced IT company. But I need to ask... if we could reduce this risk significantly and help you select the right solution, how would that impact you?"

OR

- "Transparently, this is one of the more uncomfortable parts of my job as your outsourced IT company. But I need to ask... is this a significant enough risk that we should address it now?"

OR

- "We just talked about the risk to your company—the risk of downtime, lost data, loss of company reputation. On a scale of 1-10, how major is this risk to your company?" (If it's an 8 or greater, you likely are close to a sale.)

Discover the impact to specific parts of their company (example: finance, sales, marketing, operations, etc.).

- "Tell me about your role. What do you do day-to-day?"

- "What metrics are you responsible for?"

- "Are there time-sensitive deadlines typically, like payroll has to be submitted on a specific day, or things like that?"

- "So I'm curious. If you had no access to your files or the internet, then could you access your client data or employee data?"

- "How would you do your job of <insert one or two things they just mentioned they're responsible for doing day to day> without access to your files or the internet?"

- "And if you couldn't do that, what would happen?"

(Repeat this type of question for several different "divisions" within the company.)

Discover the impact to the company, brand, or reputation.

- "What if we didn't do anything and we kept your situation the same. How do you think being down for two weeks (or more) would impact your company?"

- "How do you think your clients would react if they knew that their data got leaked in a cybersecurity incident?"

- "Would you lose any clients? How many do you think? What does that represent in terms of revenue? Is that annual or monthly?"

- "What about in terms of your sales pipeline? Do you have a robust pipeline? How much is in the pipeline right now? And you expect to close 25% of that? And what about if you had a security incident and the press found out? Would your close rate change? To what? So you'd lose X percent? What does that represent in terms of dollars?"

I hope by now you can see how rich and meaningful discovery can be. This piece of the sales process is critical—and it is *so* powerful, when done correctly.

That is because discovery isn't about you. It's about the prospect. Discovery is about helping your prospect discover the weaknesses in their company's network. It's also about helping them *feel* how those weaknesses could impact their companies if exploited.

So even if discovery feels repetitive to you, remember this is all brand new to your prospects.

I hope you now have a small idea why all the sales gurus insist that discovery is critical. Complete this part of the sales process correctly and deeply.

And then you get to the fun part—the part where you truly can ride in like a knight on a gleaming white horse and solve all their problems... because now they actually know they have them!

Never forget: *Discovery is for the prospect.*

6 | RISK MITIGATION
NOT BULLETPROOF SECURITY

Recently I attended a training led by Keenan, the author of *Gap Selling*. In that training, he talked about risk-based selling. As mentioned earlier, cybersecurity sales is selling risk mitigation, Keenan teaches that there are two factors you must consider when selling risk mitigation. Look at both these points as if you were an attorney in a high-profile court case, and you have two arguments you must prove.

The first argument is that a cybersecurity incident will be highly impactful to the organization. The second argument is that it is highly likely to happen. If you fail to prove either point, you are in the "zone of think-about-it,"

Let's look at these two arguments separately. First, you must prove that a cybersecurity incident would have a disastrous impact on the prospect's business. Once again, we are at a disadvantage, because we have lived through the reality of a cyber incident. We know firsthand how a company is affected during and after an attack. But it is important for you to remember that your clients and prospects have not walked that mile in your shoes. They have not experienced the absolute devastation, frustration, and sense of violation that come from a cybersecurity incident. It is up to you to prove that—should an incident occur—it will be highly impactful to their business.

Some of that can be done through your discovery process, which we talked about in Chapter 5. But another part of this argument should be made through your marketing. Use emails, blogs, and social media posts; share news stories of companies in your niche or in your town that have been through a ransomware incident or a breach of some type. Especially relevant are public interest pieces where a practice manager or office manager was interviewed.

These individuals will share the kinds of implications that help your prospects and clients truly understand the impact of a cybersecurity attack at the personal level—tasks like needing to bill manually or search printed files for phone numbers because electronic records weren't accessible. They will tell how their CEO or managing partner had to work 20 hours each day (for a week or more) and that they still don't know how bad the damage is or how long the CEO can keep burning the midnight oil.

This unsung hero will share how they cannot manufacture their product, track time, or bill clients. Most of all, they will share how they *felt* during the whole ordeal.

These very real stories underscore the fact that you can't simply stroke a check for $50,000 to pay the ransom and move on. Recovering from an incident is significantly more difficult than that. This is the first part of the argument you must prove to your clients and your prospects beyond any reasonable doubt: a cybersecurity incident will hurt their business.

Have you presented enough evidence to convince the jury (in this case, your prospect) that they should care about cybersecurity because of the *implications* to their business? If you have not proven your case, then you must continue the conversation because you almost certainly will not make the sale.

Now, even if you have shown the impact to the business, your job isn't done. You must now prove the likelihood that it will happen to them. This part is a bit tougher using only conversation or sharing newspaper articles, because the prospect will likely feel it can't happen to them. This is why you must perform a risk assessment. It is impossible to argue with the black and white results of a risk assessment. These results present an objective reality of their current state. Once you've performed this risk assessment, you will be able to present the prospect with clearly defined results that will make your case for you.

This should be enough to convince your prospects that—should they stay in their current unprotected or under protected state—that a significant security incident is likely to happen.

Incidentally, more than 80% of companies had a security incident in the past year. The vast majority did not know they were vulnerable— likely because they did not have a risk assessment performed.

Once your prospect realizes that an incident is highly likely to happen to them and that there is a highly probable, significant impact on their company, *then* you have enough leverage to ask for the sale. Do you tend to prove only one half of this argument? When you have proven both, then you have reached the magical place where you can Heal The Gap as noted in this illustration:

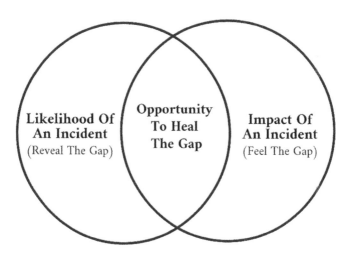

In fact, if you are debriefing your sales calls, you should add this concept to your debrief process. Ask yourself: "How well did I prove that the impact to the company would be high? Did I prove the likelihood that this would happen? Did I demonstrate risk? Did I prove these things to the prospect, or only to myself?" Start to track this paradigm, and you will see the correlation between proving risk and making the sale.

Notice that you will not promise bulletproof security. You should discuss risk mitigation. While I'm not an attorney, and you shouldn't take this as legal advice, you cannot promise something that you are not able to deliver. No one can promise bulletproof security. In fact, if you look at the NIST framework, three out of the five main points assume that there has been some type of an incident. Otherwise, there would be nothing to Detect, Respond to, or Recover from.

Recently I heard Matt Lee, CISSP, give this great analogy:

> Think of yourself as the coach of an American football team. You would never step on the field and say, "I'm never going to allow a yard." That would be stupid. It's not the reality of football, and it shouldn't be your promise when discussing cybersecurity or compliance with your prospects and clients.

> The reality is that you will allow yards, and you may even allow a touchdown. But when those things happen, you should have an incident response plan so you document the loss and how you'll improve.

Add this to your sales process! Have this conversation with your clients. Don't promise to keep the bad guys from gaining a single yard; but instead promise to put layers of protection and policies in place to reduce the likelihood that the bad guys will score a touchdown. While a gain of yardage is less than ideal, it's not game-ending.

This is a simple analogy that your clients will understand.

7 | SO WHAT?!?

I'm sure you know that in marketing, you must always answer a key question: "What's in it for me?" from the perspective of the prospect.

Well, marketing and sales are two sides of the same coin. So if it's important to answer that question in marketing, then it is equally important to answer that question in sales. This means that in every sales conversation, you must help the prospect realize what's in it for them.

Why should they care about cybersecurity? This does not mean that you should delineate a bunch of features. In their eagerness to prove the value of their cyber offer, many MSPs talk about features rather than benefits.

Your prospects won't care about features; they will only care about benefits. If you continue to drone on about aspects they don't care about, they will tune you out. But if you spell out the benefit for them, they will care deeply.

To help you differentiate between features and benefits, I teach my clients to review their selling points and ask themselves, "So what?" from the perspective of the prospect. If you must answer that question, you're likely talking about features. However, if the answer to the question is obvious, likely you're talking about a benefit.

For example, if you say to a prospect, "My solution has artificial intelligence," the prospect likely thinks, "So what? Why do I care if you have artificial intelligence? What's in it for me? I don't care how you run your business or why you selected that tool."

To find the benefit, answer the question, "So what?" As you craft your answer, keep in mind the illustration that we looked at in the previous chapter. If you can demonstrate that you are reducing risk (by reducing likelihood and reducing impact), then that is the ideal answer. That is the benefit. So perhaps your answer would be that artificial intelligence processes faster, therefore threats are much less likely to gain a foothold or do much damage. Therefore, the prospect would have less downtime because you minimized the impact to their business.

Prospects care about benefits. If you've heard the phrase, "Sell the sizzle not the steak," this is that principle at work. The sizzle represents the benefit to them—the answer to "What's in it for me?"

You must articulate the value of cybersecurity to your prospect. You must demonstrate that they should care about cybersecurity by proving that a cybersecurity incident would negatively impact their business dramatically. And if it impacts their ability to collect money, to pay their bills, to compensate their employees, to track time, to buy, to sell, to transact business, to see patients, to follow up with prospects, to manage their pipeline—and if you can reduce that risk, then you have proven the benefit to them.

Replay your latest sales call. Be critical. Analyze whether you talked about features or benefits. Did you talk about something that your prospect actually cares about? Or did you focus on techy stuff that your MSP colleagues love?

One of the biggest benefits of investing in cybersecurity is reducing the impact of a cyber incident on the prospect's business. As you have sales conversations, keep the prospect's role in the business in mind. A CEO cares about their brand and reputation, whereas the CFO cares about time tracking, billing, and revenue. A Practice Manager is concerned about how to do business during a crisis, while the Director of Sales wants to prospect and get deals signed.

So as you craft the sales conversation, paint the picture of relevant implications that the person cares about, based on the role they fill. If you can help them understand how a cyber incident could negatively impact their role, they will feel that possible pain. And remember, you must generate feelings to make the sale.

Inside the book bonuses, you'll find a list of cybersecurity implications—mapped to the role of the person who would be most impacted by that situation should a cyber incident occur. Study (or even memorize) these and show the benefit of your solution by explaining how it will minimize the likelihood of their business being impacted by such a threat.

Download your bonuses at:

MSPSalesRevolution.com/bonus

8 | YOUR HONOR, I OBJECT

No book on sales would be complete without a section about handling objections. You're skipping merrily along through your well-planned sales process, when *BAM!*... an objection is thrown your way! Your heart sinks. Your throat goes dry. You lose the ability to string a coherent sentence together.

In this chapter, let's reframe how you think about objections, as I share one of my most popular client resources.

> *Objections:* Statements or questions raised by the prospect which may indicate an unwillingness to buy

In this definition of objections, note that there is a difference between a statement and a question. Secondly, be aware that an objection *can* indicate an unwillingness to buy... but not *always*.

Let's break this down. It may seem obvious that statements are not questions. After all, you do not have to answer a statement. However, when you're on a sales call, pay close attention and remember... a statement does not require a response.

If the prospect says, "I don't know if I can buy this. It's a lot of money," that is a statement. Don't feel like you must jump right in and *overcome* that objection. Many prospects make statements to talk things through for themselves. Let them talk. Talking may be how they process information. Be comfortable letting your prospect monologue. They will often talk themselves into a sale.

Allow the prospect to talk it out for themselves.

I've made more than a dozen sales simply by letting the prospect work things out himself. If I've shown the value, the gap between where they are and where they need to be, created emotion, overcome their objections (ideally in advance), and asked for the opportunity to work together, I've done my job. I am perfectly fine waiting for the prospect to catch up to my knowledge that they should buy from me.

Every time I've done this, the prospect ends the call with this sentiment, "Thank you so much for giving me the space to figure this out. I knew *you* were convinced this was right for me. But I needed to work it out myself." You'll know you're doing something right when someone thanks you for closing a sale!

Inside the definition of objection is also the phrase, "which may indicate an unwillingness to buy." Notice the word "may." Objections *can* indicate an unwillingness to buy, but not always. Sometimes the prospect is simply asking for more information.

As salespeople, we tend to think that when a prospect raises an objection, the deal is dead. We automatically assume that it's a stop sign, as if the prospect isn't going to buy from us because of the statement they just made, or the question they just asked. It's important that we have enough emotional intelligence to understand that every time we hear an objection, it doesn't mean the prospect is unwilling or unable to buy. They are simply stating that they are not ready to buy *yet*.

I teach my MSP clients to see objections as gifts. In other words, when your prospect says to you, "I just don't see the value in your offer," or, "I don't think I need this entire stack," they are asking for more information. They are sharing a concern openly, which leaves them vulnerable. The fact that they share this with you means that they respect you and that they trust you enough to guide them. They are leaning into your expertise.

When they share a true objection with you, they're essentially asking how they can see things from your perspective. This is not a negative thing at all; this is tremendously positive. In the words of Brian Tracy, "Treat objections as requests for further information."

Think of the alternative. If they didn't trust you, they would give the dreaded, "I need to think about it," and then disappear. So by opening up, they are really asking for more information so that they can ultimately buy from you. Rather than shutting you down, they are opening up a valuable dialogue.

It's interesting to me that the prospect asks for more information and invites a conversation, yet salespeople waste time trying to "overcome the objection." I invite you to use a word other than "overcome," which implies there is a problem to be dealt with. We overcome an enemy, or we overcome our fears. But objections don't have to be negative.

The other reason I don't like the word "overcome" is that after we overcome an enemy, we have defeated them, gaining the upper hand. That's not the way I like to approach sales conversations. Instead, we want to create a partnership through sales conversations. If the partnership isn't mutually beneficial, then we shouldn't make a sales offer.

By retraining ourselves to avoid the word "overcoming" with objections, we maintain an attitude of respect and partnership.

When talking about objections, I prefer to use the word "defuse." Defusing removes the negative outcome from something. Picture a movie where the main characters are huddled around a ticking bomb. Just in the nick of time, the bomb is defused. The danger is eliminated, the stress is gone, the tension evaporates.

When we hear an objection, our goal should be to eliminate the danger, stress, and tension by defusing it. That's a completely different approach than conquering or defeating our prospect's concern.

YOUR DEFUSING TOOLBOX

Now let's learn some concrete frameworks to help defuse objections more easily.

The first is what I call the Flip-Flop Objection Defuser. With the Flip-Flop Framework, you take the concern that your prospect raised and "flip" it into the reason they should invest with you.

For example, a prospect may say, "We've never invested that much before." You will flip their concern into your answer. "That's actually the reason you need to invest with us. Do you remember how you told me about this chronic problem and that other chronic problem, and how you were worried about something specific, and how you have been waking up in the middle of the night worried about that error message you keep getting? And how you reached out to see if we could help because the frustration was more than you were willing to deal with? That's exactly why you need to work with a company like us. You won't have to worry about any of those things because you'll be investing enough to make those fears go away."

This next technique is called "Feel Felt Found." It is one of my favorites because prospects want to feel heard and understood. You are validating them when you answer in this way: "I understand how you *feel*. A lot of our clients *felt* similarly. But when they started working with us, what they *found* is that they slept better, knowing they were secure. And more than one client has thanked me for giving them peace of mind, knowing that if anything bad happened to their business, they had a plan for how to deal with it."

Apply these frameworks inside of your sales calls, and recognize that objections aren't bad. They are simply requests for additional information.

PART 4

ADVANCED
SALES CONCEPTS

9 | INSIDE THE MIND OF A SUCCESSFUL SALESPERSON

One of the principles I teach my clients is that success leaves clues. In this chapter, we will be examining clues that other successful salespeople have left behind. But you should also be aware that unsuccessful people also leave clues! This chapter will take a look at both sides of the coin.

What skills do quota-meeting salespeople have? What mindset do they cultivate? If you are a salesperson today, use these to measure yourself (and diagnose some areas for improvement). If you're hiring for a sales role, these are skills a candidate must have; otherwise you must cultivate these traits in your new employee.

We'll also take a quick look at the attitudes and behaviors of unsuccessful salespeople. Do some soul searching and evaluate your team. Correct any of these behaviors before they become habits.

COMFORTABLE WITH SALES

Successful salespeople love sales. They don't see sales as sleazy. They don't dislike the title, and they are students of sales for life. They constantly ask themselves: "How does my service or product help my prospect?" They internalize the benefits and the value of their offer. They figure out the best way to articulate their value proposition. And they spend time crafting their messaging because it supports their end goal—to help the prospect.

CONTROL FREAKS

Successful salespeople are control freaks. These people realize that they only control two things: their actions and their attitude. Everything else is out of their control and therefore not worth worrying about.

Successful salespeople realize they cannot control the fact that the prospect yelled at them, slammed down the phone, or swore in their direction. But that salesperson can control his or her attitude and response.

Perhaps today was a day where they planned to smile and dial. But they got *zero* answers. Literally 100% of calls went to voicemail. Those actions are completely out of the control of the salesperson. A seasoned pro, however, will make sure that their voicemail message is the best it can be.

 ## FRAMEWORKS

Successful salespeople have frameworks or recipes for many areas of their life. They are often freakishly focused on habits, such as their morning routine, how many dials they make per day or per week, the number of business cards they drop off, and how many networking events they attend. This is their own personal recipe for success.

They make cold calls according to a framework. This framework dictates how many calls they will make, what they will say, and how they will say it. They qualify leads in a disciplined manner. Keeping promises is a must for super stars, which means they have a framework to record promises made, and to follow up on them within deadlines.

 ## CONNECTIONS

The best salespeople are religious about meeting new people, exploring collaboration oppor-tunities, forming relationships with people in their niche and in their community, and getting to know people both in and outside their geography who are movers and shakers. They meet others for coffee. They set up Zoom meetings with new LinkedIn connections. These super stars explore partnerships. The best of the best recognize that relationships are absolute gold.

You might meet someone who becomes your biggest fan. You might meet someone who could refer you to a dozen of your most ideal prospects. Or you might find an opportunity to serve your community. Don't overlook this tip!

CURIOSITY

If you study the behavior of great salespeople, you'll see that they're curious. They think like an investigative journalist. They have an innate curiosity that permeates everything they do. They are curious about customers, their industry, their offering, and their competitors. They wonder why they made a sale or lost a deal. They're intrigued about why an objection was heard, especially if they thought they had already overcome that objection earlier in their sales call.

When you ask curiosity-induced questions, your prospects get to talk. And the more they talk, the more they like you. So leverage this tip: if you want your prospects to like you, you have to let them talk. And to let them talk, you need to be insatiably curious about everything.

Ask smart questions about their company, like why they run their business the way they do, how they're different from their competitors, how they make decisions, and more. Just do your homework beforehand, so you're not asking questions that could have been answered if you had simply browsed the prospect's website.

Asking great questions and letting the prospect talk is psychologically very powerful. Generally speaking, prospects buy from people they know, people they like, and people they trust. When you let a prospect talk about themselves, you are building "know, like, and trust" and increasing the odds that someone will buy from you.

✅ Resiliency

The part of success that nobody likes to talk about is failure. Being a salesperson is tough. You're punched in the face daily, sometimes hourly. You often have bad luck and you hear "no" exponentially more than you hear "yes."

Even if you have the right skills and frameworks, and even if you've practiced sales relentlessly, salespeople will *never* be successful 100% of the time.

The most successful salespeople get up over and over again. You cannot keep them down. They have an inner strength that is cultivated by a deep and profound belief in themself and an unyielding confidence that nothing can stop them.

They seem to bounce back much more quickly than expected. This rebound rate is important. Salespeople go through peaks and valleys. If you can "rebound" quickly from getting knocked down, you will rise to the next hill much faster than those who stay down for weeks or months.

If you lose a huge deal, are you down in the dumps for a week or two? What if you resolve to cut that number in half? And then in half again? Eventually, you'll allow yourself a grumpy hour before you get back into the fight. That is resilience; that's being mentally tough. Make that rebound rate as short as possible, and challenge yourself to make it even shorter the next time you're knocked down.

✅ GOAL SETTERS

The most successful salespeople are goal setters. They put their goals in writing. They review them every single week. They reverse-engineer these goals, so they know which actions to take to eventually achieve them. They then relentlessly push these goals forward every single day, and take actions that have a direct correlation to their goals.

RELENTLESS

Effective salespeople are relentless. Because they are super goal-oriented, they will do what it takes to reach those goals. The first way they're relentless is with follow-up. You've likely heard the phrase, "The money's in the follow-up." Well, you may have heard these words, but are you living it?

I have a friend who sells makeup. Christy is relentless about following up with me every month. She offers me mascara, lip stain, a new product, or a special bundle. She never skips a month; she is the epitome of relentless. Are you as relentless as Christy? Do you follow up with your prospects every month? Do you make sales offers on a routine basis? This is a mindset that you must cultivate.

———————————

Before I shift to talking about unsuccessful sales traits, scan back over the above eight traits. Where are you strongest? And could you make that even stronger? Where have you let things slip, due to exhaustion, lack of focus, or laziness?

After you have done some introspection, set goals to make incremental improvement. Small changes implemented consistently add up to huge gains.

What NOT to Do...

Now let's review a few traits of unsuccessful salespeople—in the hopes that you never exhibit these yourself or accidentally hire someone like this.

❌ Busy

There is a difference between actions that make you money and activity that keeps you busy. One kind of action becomes a revenue driver; the other is a vanity metric.

"Busy" is not the same as efficient. "Busy" does not mean that someone has applied Pareto's 80/20 rule—where they concentrate on the 20% of activity which drives 80% of the success—to focus on the *right* things. "Busy" doesn't mean that someone is economical with their time. "Busy" just means they are doing "stuff"... and not necessarily the right "stuff."

Many unsuccessful salespeople use a busy schedule as a status symbol. To them, having a crazy schedule is how they measure their worth. Because of this, they will never want to eliminate anything—since "busy" was the goal. Being "busy" makes them feel good.

Therefore, they make zero effort to be efficient. They don't hone their skills or create SOPs or frameworks. They want to be busy; and they want the world to know they are busy.

❌ ANYTHING FOR A SALE

Ineffective salespeople will do anything for a sale. They are willing to compromise their integrity and their honesty. They certainly don't care about your company's reputation.

Poor salespeople are willing to manipulate the prospect, as long as they close the deal, as long as they get that almighty dollar, which then equates to a commission check for them.

Some people will say and do anything to close a deal. But that's not who I want working for my company. Is that who you want working for yours?

❌ TALK. A LOT.

Unsuccessful salespeople talk exponentially more than they listen. They are so busy selling themselves and your service that they forget to listen and understand. There's no empathy there. If you step back to a time where a salesperson really got on your nerves, I bet they were talking incessantly instead of listening to your needs, concerns, and goals. They were just trying to talk you into a sale.

❌ SATISFIED

The final trait of an unsuccessful salesperson is that he or she is satisfied. They're comfortable. They aren't hungry for more. There is no desire for self-improvement. If they miss a goal, it's okay. If they completely botch a presentation, they don't strive to improve.

They don't study sales. They don't analyze their sales calls or craft great objection handling frameworks. There is no drive for more. They're satisfied. Everything's okay. They're not hungry.

———————

As you glance back at the traits of an unsuccessful salesperson, do you recognize yourself in any of them? If I stepped on your toes a little, then it's time to work on that part of your character. Because your livelihood depends on it.

10 | DON'T HIRE A SALESPERSON (YET)

Once you have a documented sales process and you start closing monthly recurring revenue (MRR) every single month, it's not unusual to consider hiring a salesperson. After all, you won't have 40 hours per week just to dedicate to sales. And every hour you spend on sales—even if you enjoy it and are good at it—is an hour you won't have to invest in strategy, management, or acquisition.

Hiring is not a bad move at this point, but there are some fundamental pieces you must have in place before making a sales hire. In fact, most MSPs who fail at hiring a salesperson missed one (or more) of these fundamentals. But you won't have to do that... because you have this chapter.

1. STRATEGY

There are different roles in sales. It's tempting to believe that you'll hire "Joe," and Joe will hunt down additional MRR. But it's important to define what Joe will do, on a day-to-day basis. Will Joe be working with your existing client base, selling those clients additional solutions? Or will Joe be working your inbound leads, to close those them as new customers? Or will Joe be focused on lead generation and networking and proposals and closing the deal?

2. DOCUMENTATION

This is the human resources side of things—the part most of us don't like. You'll need a job description, an employee agreement, and a job scorecard to track specific KPIs (Key Performance Indicators). The great thing is that as you're creating those documents, it will help you form a much more detailed concept of who you're looking for in a team member. You'll develop a far clearer idea of how much experience the right candidate should have, what kind of personality they should possess, and whether you prefer them to work from home or your office, at least initially.

3. TRACKING MECHANISM

The best way to set yourself up for success with a sales hire is to track their numbers. Sales is a numbers game. If your salesperson isn't hitting their numbers each week, they won't hit their quarterly targets. And if they do hit their numbers each week—but still miss their target—then you can analyze that same data to troubleshoot, iterate, and improve. But without a tracking mechanism, you will grow frustrated with deals that "should" close (but never do).

To be clear, you can invest in dashboard-type tools, but you can do just as well with a spreadsheet. Keep this as simple as possible to start. You can make it more complex later.

4. FAIR COMPENSATION

You must pay your team members a fair wage, maybe even on the high end of fair, so that you can acquire a really great A-player and keep them.

What does that compensation plan look like? Is it a base salary plus commission plan? Is the commission a one-time payment? Or just a bonus? Is there an ongoing commission? What's fair in your geography?

Once you establish what a fair compensation plan means for your business, you need to have enough liquid cash to pay that person for three to six months. Success in sales is never an instantaneous process. It could take 90 days or more before your salesperson closes their first sale. Without a cushion, you are financially (and emotionally) stretched.

5. ONBOARDING PLAN

Once you've hired your super star, you cannot simply throw them in the deep end and expect them to figure things out by themselves. That would be a recipe for disaster.

You'll want to plan a day-by-day agenda for their first week, an approximate daily agenda for their first month, then less frequent interaction during the second month, while the third month will include making mid-course corrections.

Be sure you teach the new hire your company culture and values, your lead-scoring systems, and your sales process. Teach them how to use your CRM and track their numbers. Have them listen to recorded sales calls—both good calls and bad ones. Then make them do some sales roleplay calls with you, so you can give them advance feedback and help them improve when the pressure is still off.

6. REALISTIC EXPECTATIONS

If you're a typical business owner, you are quite good at many things. You work quickly; you can see the end goal far off; you are resilient; you hear something one time and internalize it forever.

Those are traits of successful entrepreneur/CEO types. You're a visionary. *But that is not who you are hiring.*

Your new hire will likely move slower than you... possibly forever. Your natural instincts help you leverage automation tools, time-block your schedule, and constantly look for efficiencies. Your new hire will likely not have that background, experience, or tool set. This means that your team member may get less done in a day than you could accomplish in a few hours. However, remember that this team member is also spending 40 hours per week focused on a task you could never allocate that much time to. So be gracious and supportive.

The other thing you must anticipate is the need to repeat yourself. If your natural style is to move quickly or you easily grow impatient, chances are good that you would prefer to be able to tell your employee something one time, and never have to repeat yourself.

However, with new staff, you should expect to repeat something anywhere from 6 to 13 times before a team member realizes this is important. So once you've told your team something, and then told them again... congratulate yourself, because you only have 11 more times to go.

You should also set realistic expectations about the amount of support your new team member will need in regard to documentation. Salespeople traditionally aren't great at tracking their own numbers. Now that does not mean that you should let them off the hook. It simply means that you must provide support systems to help them learn to keep better documentation, while also making them aware that your company is driven by numbers and they will be held accountable.

7. CUSTOMER RELATIONSHIP MANAGEMENT (CRM) TOOL

While you likely have a ticketing tool, new hires are usually not great when it comes to managing marketing and sales. As you hire a salesperson, you must have a tool in place to fuel their sales efforts, stay organized, and track activities. Three common favorites are ActiveCampaign, Keap (formerly Infusionsoft), and Hubspot. There are many to choose from. Pick one and learn it, and make sure your sales team completes the training needed.

8. NAMES

To set up a salesperson for success, you need names of new leads. Determine the number of qualified prospects in your area (the Total Addressable Market) and get those names!

Some of these prospects will naturally enter your ecosystem—having downloaded your website's lead magnet, through meeting you at a networking event, or having attended a webinar—but most prospects will not reach out to you proactively. Be sure you have a strategy to grow this list; and then engage those companies.

The largest MSPs have an entire team member or virtual assistant dedicated to tracking down those names. Afterward, another team member warms up those names by inviting them to events. Ultimately, the names can be handed to your salesperson to nurture and close.

9. DOCUMENTED SALES PROCESS

As you learned in Chapter 4, companies with documented sales processes close more deals. Before you hire a salesperson, make sure you've documented what works for your company, scripts, and ways to defuse objections. You could create a fancy, detailed process map, or you could simply have a checklist. Either way, set your salesperson up for success by providing this valuable document.

10. TIME

The most important thing you need to have in place before hiring a salesperson is your time. You will need time to prep new-hire documentation. Time to manage them. Time to onboard them. Time to fix challenges. Time to troubleshoot processes you never needed before. And time to chat about nothing so you can just get to know the person!

Understand that in the first few months of employment, the new hire will *cost* you time. You need to emotionally accept this fact and plan time up front that will help you set this employee up for success. In the long run, you both will benefit.

11 | NEVER CLOSE
ANOTHER SALE AGAIN

There have been many blogs, webinars, and books written about closing the sale. Many salespeople search for the magic words that will allow them to compel a buyer to invest in their solution.

Common search terms related to "closing a sale" include "tips to close a sale," "how to close a sale," "unique approach to closing a sale," "secrets of closing a sale," and "closing a sale faster."

I'm here to set the record straight: these are all the wrong search strings. If you are hoping for that illusive trick or technique to unlock a magical spell for "easy sales" (maybe you even skipped ahead to this chapter without reading what came before), well, I hate to break it to you... but we aren't living in a Harry Potter movie. There is no point in time where you can wave a magic wand, speak a series of magic words, and cause the prospect to suddenly see the wisdom in your cybersecurity value proposition.

Perhaps you've bought into the notion that closing is one of a few critical (or perhaps *preeminent*) qualities of a successful salesperson. When considering the quality of a potential sales hire, you may have heard yourself ask, "But can this person *close?*" You may even recognize that your self-confidence is impacted when you're in a slump.

> *"Closing" is not the last 3-5 minutes of a sales call... it starts the first moment you meet.*

Many sales trainers focus on "closing" as if it were a separate and discrete portion of the interaction with a prospect when you have suddenly arrived at a specific point in time when you are somehow allowed to begin closing the deal. The term "closing" is misleading because it suggests an ending, or a finality. In reality, once the sale is made, the relationship is just beginning.

Indeed, if you had to pinpoint the moment that the buyer agreed with the conditions of the sale and made a commitment to moving forward, you would be stuck. There is no single moment when this happens.

You might be able to cite a specific moment where the prospect said, "We have a deal." But you'll never spot the precise moment where the prospect emotionally connected with the vision you painted of the future state. There will not be a single split-second that solidified trust between you and the prospect. You won't be able to extract this specific point in time because *closing is done throughout the selling process.*

In short, closing is a journey. If you picture the typical MSP sales stages, you will see something like this:

1. Prospect calls or fills out a form
2. Qualification call
3. Initial (discovery) meeting
4. Risk assessment completed
5. Risk assessment result meeting / agreement signed

Let's assume that the prospect interacts with you for only three hours of face-to-face selling time. You are weaving discovery, storytelling, and information sharing into that process. You're dodging preconceived notions and juggling the personalities of several decision makers. Do you really believe that the sale is made in the three to five minutes near the end of Step 5? That's just silly!

Now if you flipped straight to this chapter hoping I'd reveal the secret to end all sales secrets, you're still in good hands. It's not a magic "spell" that will perfect those last critical minutes before signing an agreement. That's not the way sales works. *But...* I will reveal the secret... in a few minutes.

I want you to look at this another way. Let's say you came home from the office today. You opened the door, and you smelled fresh baked cookies! Your spouse/best friend/favorite child timed it perfectly, and they hand you an ooey, gooey cookie. Your favorite kind—exactly the right mix of crunchy and chewy. Do you think, *Wow! When did we get the magical oven that spits out cookies?* Or do you instead look to your loved one and say, "Thank you so much for making me cookies!"

You see, cookie making is a process. It requires a specific set of ingredients. If you want the cookies to be perfect, you must follow the recipe. When you taste the fabulous cookie hot out of the oven, you realize that you're tasting the result of a complex process.

If you are unhappy with the results of your cookie, you need to change the cookie-making process. Likewise, if you're unhappy with your closing rates, you must change your sales process.

Closing is not a single point in time. Closing is a *cumulative* effort. It is (or should be) happening all the way through your sales calls.

It's like the game of American football. Scoring a touchdown must be accomplished one yard at a time. We keep score using the touchdown. It's the most critical metric. But scoring a touchdown would be impossible without the cumulative effort of play after play where the team gains a yard (and sometimes even loses a few yards).

There is no magic spell to make a football team score more touchdowns. The "formula" is to follow the coaching playbook, study what works, perfect what isn't quite right, iterate, and thus improve. All of those steps combined make the touchdown almost an afterthought.

A "touchdown" in sales must be scored "yard by yard."

If you approach football by asking "how do I get more touchdowns" or "secrets to getting touchdowns" or "getting to the end zone faster" then you're playing football wrong. The way to score more points in football is to play the entire game better.

Therefore "closing" is simply part of the entire sales process. It is the natural progression of gains made "one yard at a time." It starts at the beginning of your first appointment.

- You must close your prospect on deciding something at the end of the sales call.

- You must close the prospect on the need for a risk assessment.

- You must close the owner on why cybersecurity matters.

- You must close the decision makers on risk mitigation.

- You must close the decision makers on why they should show up to see the result of your risk assessment.

- You must close your prospect on making a buying decision at the end of the final sales call.

- You must use tie-downs and micro-commitments throughout your sales calls.

All of this is *closing*! That's why picturing "closing" as a single point in time (at the very end of your sales call) is incorrect. "Closing" must be done throughout every sales interaction. When done correctly, your "closing question" can literally be,

"We've talked about a lot of risk today, and you agreed it wasn't something you were willing to absorb. I know we can help. Will you please let us?"

Use this single principle, and you'll never have to close a sale again. They'll practically close themselves.

12 | TELL ME A STORY!

Storytelling is one of the most powerful tools a successful salesperson has in their toolbelt. Storytelling is one of the best ways to influence, teach, and inspire. If you weave a few stories into your sales calls, they will make up for a multitude of techno-babble geek speak.

Stories are especially effective when you get stuck being one of three MSPs that your prospect is meeting. Unless you are the last MSP on the list, it's difficult to achieve a one-call close. Chances are your prospect will be talking to a competitor in a few days or weeks and you will become a victim of "The Forgetting Curve."

THE FORGETTING CURVE

It's the reality that your very human prospects will forget about half of your presentation within an hour. And the next day? They'll remember (at best) 30% of what you said. A week later, they've forgotten 90% of what you shared.

Research by cognitive psychologist Jerome Bruner suggests that a message delivered as a story can be up to 22 times more memorable than just facts. Stories engage the emotions of your listener and keep their attention. Stories are engaging.

Armed with this information, why not decide precisely which points you want your prospects to remember by crafting a compelling story to drive home each point? In other words, take your newfound understanding of human psychology, count on your competitors' ignorance of this knowledge, and then engineer your sales process so that your prospects can't help but remember your stories.

THIS IS YOUR BRAIN ON... OXYTOCIN

Beyond helping your prospects remember your message, stories have another superpower. Stories help us feel a greater sense of connection to one another. When we hear a story, our brain releases oxytocin, a hormone known as the bonding or love hormone. Some researchers call this the "trust hormone." We know that prospects buy from people they know, like, and trust. So why not engineer your sales process in such a way that your prospects can't help but like you and trust you?

PROSPECTS BUY EMOTIONALLY

The reality is that your prospects do not buy *features* and *benefits*. They buy emotions. Almost no one will lean in to learn more about your latest AI machine-learning gadget. Emotion is what drives purchasing behaviors (and decision making in general).

Neuroscientists have learned that people whose brains are damaged in the area that generates emotions are incapable of making decisions. Even simple decisions like what to wear to work become impossible for these people. Without emotions, there is zero decision-making ability.

When salespeople talk in black and white (facts, data, analysis, and features) only two parts of people's brains are engaged. But as soon as a salesperson adds people, places, and stories to that raw data, the brain lights up in seven places!

Stories are engaging; data and pitches are not. You know what's coming, right? Stories generate emotions. So craft stories that encourage your prospect to buy from you.

STORIES: THE NEXT STEP

All stories (including those used by salespeople) have a beginning, a middle, and an end. They are about a person (or group) who encounters an obstacle and overcomes that challenge. If you're familiar with Donald Miller's book, *Building a Story Brand,* then this framework should sound familiar. The hero's journey (where the audience is the hero) is the basis of every great story.

Your job is to craft an arsenal of great stories and then memorize them. And use them at the ideal time. Use this simple checklist to get the juices flowing. Remember to include these three elements: (1) Person or group; (2) Who encounter a challenge; and (3) How they overcame the challenge.

- A story about the not-for-profit board member who found a great cybersecurity plan but couldn't get the board's approval. This sad story tells how a later cyber incident impacted them and what happened after they partnered with you.

- A sad narrative that relates the end of the story after someone declined to adopt your cybersecurity offer.

- A take-your-breath-away-tale of a CEO who bit the bullet, spent more than he wanted to, and just barely avoided a disaster.

- A sad story about a CFO who *thought* she was doing the right thing by buying a budget cybersecurity offer.

- A story of a current customer who invested in your offer, and what happened then.

Don't overlook the power of the above framework. The time you invest to create powerful stories will pay amazing dividends. You'll start to see this framework in stories, movies, and even in objection handling techniques! For example, the common technique "Feel Felt Found" is story telling reworked.

"I completely understand how you **feel**.	(group of people)
Some of our other clients **felt** exactly the same way.	(encountered a challenge)
What they **found** was..."	(they overcame the challenge, with your help)

Story telling is such a fun tool—and one that you'll want to spend time perfecting. Since you want to influence your prospects to adopt your solution and your way of thinking, craft stories. Use them liberally, and perhaps even track and measure their effectiveness. I think you'll grow to love this tip!

PART 5

THE PATH
FORWARD

13 | HOW I HELP MSPs GROW THEIR BUSINESSES

———————|———————

I hope by now you can see that selling cybersecurity is not only possible but easy, when following the right structure. You've also had the belief reinforced that you *must* sell cybersecurity to your marketplace. To do anything else is a disservice to your clients, and a significant business risk to you.

I started coaching my first MSP on cybersecurity sales in 2016, as part of a small cybersecurity startup CARVIR. After we were acquired by Continuum, I continued to train MSPs on the best ways to market and sell cybersecurity.

So many of my life experiences have converged into what I do now. From running the sales and marketing efforts for my husband's MSP, to training with CharTec and TruMethods, to working at Technology Marketing Toolkit where I coached almost 1,000 MSPs on best practices related to sales and marketing, to coaching MSPs on cybersecurity sales at a startup.

Through those experiences, I have been able to hone my training abilities, and in 2019, I created my own boutique mentorship firm, *MSP Sales Revolution*. In my company, we focus on helping MSPs with $700,000 to $7M in annual revenue, and we help them create "catastrophic" success. We know that as these already successful companies grow, they will encounter new challenges, which initially look like disasters. But we have the tools and support systems in place to guide our clients through these challenges and mentor them to rise to even greater levels of success.

HOW MSP SALES REVOLUTION IS UNIQUE:

We work with the top 20% of our industry. Some say that our approach is silly and that we limit ourselves. In fact, many coaching programs focus on emerging 6-figure companies while simultaneously marketing to startups. This approach violates fundamental marketing principles, which demand focus.

But beyond this fact, there are other reasons we focus on this specific group of MSPs.

1. *We want to stay small.* Focusing on the cream of the crop allows us to do that. We keep our client base far below 100 MSP clients because our hearts' desire is to make a *significant* difference in the lives (and businesses) of our clients. We simply cannot deliver a true mentorship experience if we have hundreds (or thousands) of clients.

   One of the favorite parts of my week is when a client reaches out asking, "Can we have a quick 20-minute call so I can be 100% prepared for tomorrow's sales call?" Or "I just majorly bombed on my sales call. Can we talk?" Or "I need to figure out what my next hire is going to be. Can you act as a sounding board for me and my executive team?" The answer is a resounding *YES*—which I could never do if I had a larger client base.

2. *Success breeds success.* We love partnering with companies who execute—and our clients love being surrounded by others who are driven to succeed. Generally speaking, companies with a team, even a team of 4, are more focused and disciplined than startups. Our clients receive guidance, and then they go execute. If they get stuck, they reach out for advice, receive it quickly, and run to the next

challenge. They identify business obstacles, and they actively work to solve them. They (rarely) make excuses. This generates a culture of success, and is a rising tide for all involved.

3. *Vision.* Each of our clients has a different vision for their company. Some want a multi-state business—with the goal of being acquired someday. Others want to create a business that fuels their ideal life (perhaps saving for an early retirement, a boat or vacation experience, or so they can take weeks off to focus on passion projects). We've found that during the busyness of business, it's easy to lose that vision... to go off course. We help our clients install a "GPS" of sorts, so they are driving toward *their* end goal, not one that the gurus tout as being the holy grail.

ABOUT PEAK PERFORMANCE

We are privileged to work with a small group of MSPs in our Peak Performance mentorship. A mentorship is what you get if you combine group coaching and 1-on-1 consulting.

We help our clients install a proven lead generation and sales system into their companies. That way they can add new profitable clients every month.

Our Peak Performance mentorship program is based on the SMART system.

S = Sales. Nothing happens until you make a sale. But that demands that you have a proven, documented sales process. You'll get that process, and the deep psychology behind it, inside of our mentorship. Sales is a muscle which atrophies without constant attention. Because many MSPs only have a handful of sales calls per month, you'll get a place to practice sales calls in advance and troubleshoot sales calls after they conclude.

M = Marketing. You can be the best salesperson in the universe, yet you'll never make a sale if you don't have leads. Inside of Peak Performance, you'll focus on sane, scalable marketing strategies. You'll learn what works so you can install a proven lead generation system in your business.

A = Accountability. Many of our clients are excellent leaders who expect high output from their team. But those leaders sometimes lose focus on their own task list. They find that the *urgent* tasks often bleed into the *important* tasks. We are the guide that highlights promises made, but not kept; goals set but forgotten about; annual goals that are gathering dust in a long-forgotten planning document. We are the gentle nudge (or, for our more stubborn clients, the firm kick in the rear) that reminds you to focus on *your* version of success.

R = Recurring Revenue. Of course MRR is the holy grail for MSPs. But we focus on *profitable* sales. As a growing leader, you need to know how to read financials. Of course, knowing how to pull a P&L isn't enough. You must be able to spot trends, opportunities, and challenges. You'll get this guidance, applied to your business practically and simply, so you can grow the business of your dreams.

T = Time. I'd wager that everyone reading this book has heard the maxim, "Work *on* your business, not *in* your business." But beyond that motto, there is very little practical training available. Inside of Peak Performance, you'll learn a framework which will help you identify what has been stealing your time, and you'll learn how to put these thieves in jail where they belong—thus freeing you to pursue your dream.

14 | THE NEXT STEP

Congratulations! You have taken a *huge* step toward creating a cybersecurity sales process for your MSP. You can now approach all future sales calls with the knowledge that you are helping other people and their businesses to avoid the pain and financial devastation that often accompany cybersecurity attacks. You are confident that selling your prospects and current clients cybersecurity services means you offer them not only peace of mind, but also mitigate risk of a future that could bring their business crashing to an abrupt end.

I hope I've opened your eyes to how simple it is to sell cybersecurity, and that you're excited about mitigating risk for your clients. You may even be excited about the potential of us working together, practicing these skills in real life, and growing your cybersecurity revenue.

Imagine what it would feel like to walk into a sales call with full confidence, knowing without a doubt that you are prepared for any conversation, including the objections!

Think about the satisfaction you'll feel as you close profitable cybersecurity deals and watch the business of your dreams unfold right before your eyes.

Trust me. Those feelings are real, and they make the struggles—and all the ups and downs—completely worthwhile.

You can certainly apply these principles yourself, but together we can help you implement them faster and better.

KEEP ON SWIMMING

If you like what you've read so far and feel like working with me to accelerate your success makes sense, let me ask you to carefully consider (and answer) a few questions:

1. Would you be a better security-minded salesperson if you worked closely with me for 3 months, 6 months, or a year?

2. Are you serious about growing your dream business now?

3. Do you value working with an expert to guide you, bring out the best in you, give you confidence, and prevent mistakes?

If you answered yes to all of those, then you have a couple of choices, and I encourage you to choose now.

1. You can close this book. Recognize that you *could* work with me to speed up your success, but for a reason known only to you, you really want to attempt the DIY (Do It Yourself) method first. (If that's the route you take, I truly hope it goes better than my DIY dishwasher repair where I managed to flood my basement...)

2. You can prevent countless false starts and mistakes with executing the truths in this book, and schedule a *Cybersecurity Sales Strategy Session* with me to discuss your current approach to closing sales and growing your business.

If you're serious about protecting your clients— NOW—then you have nothing to lose by choosing the second option.

This one call can unlock your greatness and show you the path toward becoming a sales rockstar!

There's no obligation, and scheduling it is super easy.

Your goals and timeline are unique to you, which is why we need to chat—if you're serious about selling cybersecurity and growing your business.

This call is all about showing you where you rank for each element of our SMART system. We'll decide if it makes sense to work together to improve your ranking.

Maybe we're meant to work together, and maybe not. You'll never know if we never have this first, critical conversation.

SEIZE THE DAY. TODAY.

Will you learn how to sell cybersecurity profitably, easily, and confidently?

Your current clients, your future clients, and your future self are waiting just around the corner for you. This is your call-to-action and my challenge to you.

I challenge you to answer the call.

I challenge you to step into your greatness.

I promise... you are ready!

Schedule your *Cybersecurity Sales Strategy Session* with me now. There's no fee, no obligation, no risk, nothing to lose... and everything to gain.

HOW TO SCHEDULE OUR CALL

Visit **MSPSalesRevolution.com/unlock**

If you are ready to unlock the sales genius inside of you, this is the time.

Watch the video on the page to refresh your memory on how I work with companies.

Click the *Strategy Session* button and schedule a call with me.

I look forward to hearing from you—and more importantly, working together to unlock the cybersecurity sales genius inside of you and helping you create the business of your dreams.

Thank you!

~Jennifer

BONUS RESOURCES

As a special "thank you gift" for my readers,
I'm sharing some extra resources
to make it even simpler for you
to sell cybersecurity!

Previously for private clients only,
now you can get access, too.

Download Your Special
Reader Bonus Now:

MSPSalesRevolution.com/Bonus

ABOUT THE AUTHOR

JENNIFER BLEAM is a wife, the mother of three boys, and a mentor for MSPs looking to dominate their marketplace and build the company of their dreams.

Throughout her 3 decades in the marketing and sales world (and 2 decades in the IT industry), Jennifer has been a student of marketing and sales. She firmly believes that knowledge isn't power; applying that knowledge is power. She has consistently applied the lessons learned from hundreds of books and great business leaders like Dan Kennedy and Darren Hardy. Those lessons have allowed her to surpass normal expectations and outcomes.

Her drive and expertise have led her to grow several multi million dollar companies and divisions in under 2 years each. She's been featured in countless trade publications and podcasts and has been a guest speaker and trainer on stages around the world including North America, Australia, and Europe. To date, Jennifer has coached over 2,000 MSPs on effective sales and marketing to small and medium sized businesses.

In 2019, Jennifer launched MSP Sales Revolution, a boutique mentorship founded on her proven principles of hard work, marketing strategy, and consistent execution. This formula works for any IT firm with at least $60k in MRR!

Jennifer is also the administrator of the largest Facebook group dedicated to cybersecurity sales, where she interviews cybersecurity vendors and thought leaders from the industry to help MSP businesses scale.

To learn more about Jennifer and her company, visit www.MSPSalesRevolution.com. And if you're looking for a content-rich, dynamic speaker for your event, podcast, or webinar, contact Jennifer for her speaker kit.

A SMALL REQUEST

Thank you for reading *Simplified Cybersecurity Sales for MSPs*. I am positive that if you follow what I've written, you will become even more successful at selling cybersecurity services.

I have a small (and quick) favor to ask. Would you mind taking a couple of minutes and leaving an honest review for this book on Amazon, Goodreads, or another platform? Reviews are the *best* way to help others decide whether or not to purchase this book, and I check all my reviews looking for suggestions I can incorporate in the next version of my book.

Thanks!

Made in the USA
Las Vegas, NV
14 December 2022

62386623R00085